10 Ways to Insulate your Relationship

10 Ways to Insulate your Relationship
by Diane McDaniel

Published by Diane N. McDaniel.

Printing History:

May 2007:   First Edition

ISBN: 978-0-6151-4946-2

Acknowledgements

To my husband Paul, thank you for choosing me to spend the rest of your life with. I would not have been able to share these gems of wisdom if I was not married to you.

10 Ways to Insulate your Relationship

Contents

10 Ways to Insulate your Relationship

About the Author

Diane McDaniel is happily married and lives in New Jersey, USA. She graduated from Camden County College in Blackwood, New Jersey, where she took counseling and psychology classes as electives. She is currently working full time and also pursuing a bachelor's degree in Computer Science at Rutgers State University in New Brunswick, New Jersey. Diane McDaniel is also a volunteer as a mentor with Icouldbe.org.

10 Ways to Insulate your Relationship

Introduction

It is extremely challenging to maintain a healthy relationship, in this day and age, because there are so many distractions. Years go by and you realize that you are not spending quality time with your partner, due to the fact that you have let too many things interfere with your relationship. Gradually, your significant other, the person that you once knew so well becomes a stranger.

In this book I am going to point out 10 ways you can shield your relationship from external interference.

I trust that you will find this book useful and may it prompt you to implement the necessary changes in your relationship to make it healthy and strong. I believe that healthy relationships build peaceful communities, which in turn are the foundation for peaceful nations, and it is only after we build peaceful nations can we attain world peace.

The Workplace

Ninety percent of all affairs begin in the workplace, because it is where we spend most of our time. Let me put things into perspective to show you approximately how much time you spend at home. After an eight-hour workday, you spend maybe about <u>four</u> hours awake when you get home, and then you sleep the rest of the night.

My hypothesis is that when two people of the opposite sex spend a lot of time together they end up developing feelings for each other, regardless of their physical appearance. This is precisely how affairs begin in the work place.

The most effective way to prevent temptation in the office is to refrain from spending too much time with one person of the opposite sex. For example, you can avoid having lunch with one individual of the opposite sex everyday by going out to lunch with a group of your co-workers. If for some reason you have to spend your lunch hour with that one person every single day, like in the case where you work in a very small office, then steer clear from sharing personal issues that you should be sharing with your partner. Also, call your significant other during your lunch hour and be open about who you are having lunch with. You can even take this a step further and introduce your partner to your co-worker over the phone if they have never met before.

Once you introduce your lunch buddy to your partner, this acts as a deterrent to cross the line with them, and vice versa.

Also, for those days when you have to work late with your boss or a co-worker of the opposite sex, make sure you check in with your partner periodically. It is also a good practice to display pictures of your significant other on your desk.   The pictures serve as a reminder to you that you are accountable to your partner for your actions and thoughts. Remember, if you work long hours, your brain gets exhausted which in turn can cause impaired judgment and you can make decisions that you may regret later.   In addition, when you have to meet deadlines you can always take your work home with you; although, I do not recommend you do this if you have kids.

So you followed all the above tips and you still find yourself attracted to that new co-worker, but do not worry, because this is just a temporary infatuation that can be easily reversed. Think back to when you first met your partner and they seemed perfect, because your focus then was solely on their looks, but once you got to really know them you discovered that they have weaknesses, faults and irritating habits. Well, the person you are fascinated with is only tempting because you do not yet know everything about them. Once you get to know them they may not be that attractive. Please let this reality set in and try to get over the temporary infatuation.

1. What immediate steps can you take to prevent temptations in the workplace?

The Internet

I am a huge advocate of technological advances and my passion completely lies with Information Technology. However, there is always a negative side to a positive innovation.

The Internet has played a very positive role in globalization and making the world a smaller place when it comes to communication. People are now able to communicate across continents and oceans just by the click of a mouse. On the other hand, the Internet has also become a media that partners use to cheat on each other; this is where people tend to have emotional affairs and even what is now known as cyber sex. This kind of cheating is just as bad or even worse than physical affairs.

Since you know all the details about how the affairs start and how they are carried out, I will focus on how you can insulate your relationship from this type of intrusion.

Firstly, I strongly recommend that couples have the same e-mail address, so that both can have access to incoming and outgoing e-mails. I know you may oppose this idea because you think you will lose your individuality and you need your own privacy and space, however, the problem is that a lot of people abuse this privacy. There are so many temptations in cyber space that if you share the same e-mail then your relationship will be affair proof.

Secondly, if the idea of having the same e-mail address is a little too much, then you can continue to have separate e-mail addresses but exchange passwords. This does not mean that you should read your partner's e-mails everyday, but if you suspect anything you will be able to go in and investigate. Also, just knowing that your partner has the password to your e-mail address will prevent you from taking part in any inappropriate correspondence.

So you are saying to yourself how about instant messages? Unfortunately, if you are not computer savvy, you many not be able to track instant messages. I suggest that you keep the computer in the open and be alert if your partner is up all night doing "work" on the computer. I am not suggesting that you should look over your partner's shoulder each time they turn on the computer, but just follow your gut instinct, because we human beings have a way of sensing when something is not right.

Thirdly, after you are in a serious relationship you both need to notify ex-lovers about your commitment, delete their e-mail addresses and pretty much stop communicating with them when you are not with your partner. Even though they were a part of your life before, now your partner is a part of your life, what do you need your ex for? Except if you share a child, there is really no need to communicate. The only other exception is if you work together. The thing is if you correspond with ex lovers the main thing you will be doing is flirting, and some affairs start with a simple flirt.

Aside from actually having an emotional affair via e-mail or chatting, spending too much time on the Internet is also not good for your relationship. The focus should be on spending time together and not surfing the net. Some couples spend very little time communicating because one of them is constantly surfing the web.

The time spent on the Internet needs to be balanced in order to have a healthy and strong relationship.

2. How much time do you spend on the Internet? Do you think this is a reasonable amount of time? Why or why not? Would you visit the same websites if your significant other was in the room?

Friends

Sadly, we do not realize that making a serious commitment means that our lifestyle has to change. We get excited about the idea of committing to a relationship; however, we want everything else to stay the same.

As much as we love our friends, they can be a main source of disagreement in a relationship.

Sometimes friends may cause us to spend less time building our relationship with our partners. This is especially true for men. I say this because once women fall in love they tend to spend most of their time with their partners and they are quick to tell their girlfriends "sorry I won't be able to make it". However, guys never want to come across as weak to their friends, so they continue to hang out till all hours of the night, even after they get into a serious relationship. This sort of behavior could create a distance between couples.

Once you are in a serious relationship, your partner should be the number one priority before your friends, so the guys' night out should be mutually agreed upon. Furthermore, the time spent hanging out with the guys has to be reasonable. Also, ladies the same thing applies to you and the time you spend with your girlfriends.

The best way to circumvent friends being a source of conflict in your relationship is by trying to associate with friends that are in committed relationships, because they will be more responsible with the time they spend with you.

3. Do you think your friends are causing disagreements in your relationship? Identify ways you can mutually agree on the time that should be spent with friends.

Dreams

By dreams I am not referring to dreams that you have when you go to bed at night, am referring to dreams that we pursue in our lifetime.

There are people who are extremely passionate about what they want to achieve in life, hence, they tend to be highly driven and spend every waking moment pursuing their dreams.

This can also be a source of conflict in a relationship. The question here is why would you ask someone to spend the rest of their life with you, only to put them on standby while you completely ignore their needs and pursue your dreams?

In order to keep a relationship going strong, our individual dreams and passions have to come second.

In a relationship you have to balance the time spent pursuing dreams in order to make sure that your partner does not feel neglected, otherwise you will end up losing the best thing that ever happened to you.

4. Do you spend most of your time pursuing your dreams? How can you balance the time so your partner does not feel neglected in the process?

Video Games

Every woman can identify with this recent electronic craze. Unfortunately, guys this topic is going to be hard on you. Kids have literally stopped going outside to play because of these little gadgets. There are young and "old" kids completely obsessed with video games today.

This is an addiction that has not been classified as such; therefore, there is no hotline for video game anonymous, no support group and no therapy. Also, since this has not been recognized as an addiction, it is going to take a long time before any sort of help in available.

Some men tend to spend way too much time playing video games and miss out on everyday life. Video games cause them to pay no attention to their partners because one hundred percent of their focus is given to these electronic gadgets.

Ladies, if your partner picks up a video game as soon as he steps into the house, if he gives you only half of his attention and if he stays up all night trying to get to level one hundred and gets defensive when you bring it up, then yes these are signs of video game addiction! Nonetheless, do not lose hope because all is not lost, sit down with him, if possible away from the house and the video game, and be honest with him about how you feel. If you do not honestly express yourself about this, subsequently you will resent the video game and eventually resent him and this will slowly destroy everything you have built together.

I am not implying that video games are bad, to the contrary, because the benefits are that they stimulate the mind and help people develop amazing hand eye coordination, but there has to be a balance.

Due to the fact that your partner will play these games with his buddies, if this issue is not addressed quickly, then slowly his buddies become more important to him than you, because they will obsess over the games twenty-four hours. If the time spent playing video games is not kept in balance, then this can be a complete love buster.

5. If you are obsessed with video games, what steps can you take to cut back? Would you consider doing other activities that you can both enjoy?

Family and Relatives

Let me paint a small picture for you, imagine that you lived with your parents and siblings up to the time when you decided to get into a serious relationship. Probably the only time you left home was when you went to college and then you came right back. On the day you decide to move out, your family and relatives are happy for you; but, it does not sink into their minds that since you have your own place, you will not be 'home' that much. I say 'home' because your new place with your partner is essentially now your home, and the home you were used to is now your parent's house. So as you can see things change and your family and relatives need to realize this.

It is impossible to spend the same amount of time at 'home' and still be able to build on your new relationship. Being committed means that your partner becomes your number one priority. I stress this point because a lot of people do not really think of it this way; they flip the order of things and think that parents and siblings come first before their partners.

As much as we love our biological families, they can also be a source of hindering growth in relationships. Hence, you have to take a stance and establish boundaries, because this will bring about respect and give you room to work on your new relationship and make it grow.

6. Do your parents and siblings come first before your significant other? What necessary steps can you take to reverse this order of priorities?

Television

Television can be a great source of information, entertainment and education if used appropriately.

However, most of us misuse this device. Ask yourself how much time you spend watching television, and compare this to the time you spend talking with your partner.

We spend hours, sitting on the sofa side by side, watching television and completely forget that the other person is sitting right next to us.

Television can be a passive distraction for any relationship. If the time spent watching TV is not controlled, then one day you will realize that you really do not even know your partner.

Turn the TV off once in a while and have meaningful conversations, especially during meals, and if possible do not put a television set in your bedroom.

Also, we sometimes get so engrossed in television programs that we start to identify with the different characters, but what we need to remember is that they are not our reality, but our partners are real. We cannot talk, laugh with and touch the people we see on TV everyday, but we can talk, laugh with and touch our partners. Bear in mind that everything in life needs to have a balance.

7. How much time do you spend watching television in a day? If you spend more than three hours straight, what shows can you give up to spend quality time with the one you love?

Kids

This chapter is specifically for you ladies.

It is sad to think that our bundles of joy can cause division in a relationship, but it has happened.

Women have a tendency of shifting their focus, from the husband to the baby, after having kids. This may seem like the right thing to do as a mother, but, before the baby your partner was your priority and all of a sudden you expect them to take a back sit while they watch you hover over the baby all the time. Keep in mind that the baby needs an emotionally healthy dad, and a neglected dad will be no good to your child.

Ladies, we have to maintain a balance; love the baby, but, definitely do not neglect your partner. Make time to get away with your partner, find a baby sitter or a relative to watch the baby so the two of you can spend quality time together. This will strengthen your relationship, even after you have kids, and will give the children emotionally happy parents.

8. Find a baby sitter for one weekend a month and the two of you should spend quality time alone. Write down a list of people you trust to baby sit and call them to see if they are available.

Work

We all need to work to make ends meet. On the other hand, if working all the overtime and taking work home with you is going to destroy your relationship, then I suppose you need to cut back. It is important that we give work our all, but, try to do it just for eight hours that you have to be there, life is not all about work. If your income is not enough and you have to work two jobs, then try to find a better paying job so you can only work one job, or consider a change of profession.

We have to be creative and find ways to balance work and leisure. Keep your priorities in order, so that your partner does not feel like they come second to your career goals.

The best way to balance time spent at work is to ask your manager for flex time. Moreover, make sure that your work hours match your partner's, so that you are both home at the same time and you could probably car pool and eat breakfast together. Remember, the focus here is to spend as much quality time together as you can, life is short so do not let work be your life.

9. Are you spending too much time at work? What can you do to change this? If you work two or more jobs find out what you can do to increase your income without having to work more than one job. Do you have a business idea you have been putting off?

Hobbies

The ideal situation would be to have the same hobbies, but we all know that this only happens in a perfect world and we live in an imperfect world.

Most of the time you will have completely different hobbies from each other, nevertheless, the important thing is not to let your hobbies consume too much of your time.

For example, my main hobby is reading, and this is not my husband's hobby. My problem is that when I pick up a book, I get completely engrossed in it; hours can go by without me even looking up. Before I got married this was acceptable, but now that am married I have to make sure that I put the book down once in a while, no matter how good the story is, and check on my husband. As a result, now it takes me about a week or two to finish a book that I would have read in one day during my single years, but that is all right, because no novel on earth is more important than my partner.

If you occupy yourself attending to your hobbies and ignoring your partner, then your relationship will be in jeopardy. Therefore, keep it under control and try as much as you can to balance your time.

10. List down your hobbies, if you have more than one, and from that list think of a way to cut back on the time spent on them.

Notes

Notes

Notes

Notes

_____

www.ingramcontent.com/pod-product-compliance
Lightning Source LLC
Chambersburg PA
CBHW032035090426
42741CB00006B/832